CW00642562

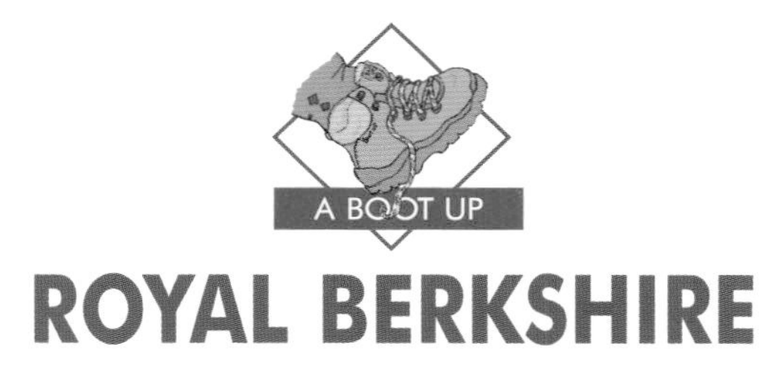

ROYAL BERKSHIRE

Mike Cope

First published in Great Britain in 2011

British Library Cataloguing-in-Publication Data
A CIP record for this title is available from the British Library

ISBN 978 0 85710 042 9

PiXZ Books
Halsgrove House, Ryelands Business Park,
Bagley Road, Wellington, Somerset TA21 9PZ
Tel: 01823 653777
Fax: 01823 216796
email: sales@halsgrove.com

An imprint of Halstar Ltd, part of the Halsgrove group of companies
Information on all Halsgrove titles is available at: www.halsgrove.com

Printed and bound in China by Toppan Leefung Printing Ltd

Contents

How to use this book

The Area

The county of Berkshire is bordered by Oxfordshire, Surrey, Hampshire, Buckinghamshire and Wiltshire, and its county town is Reading. The majority of its northern boundary is formed by the River Thames, which has played a part in the original formation of the county. Since the nineteenth century, it has been referred to as a royal shire due to the presence of a royal residence, Windsor Castle, in the north east of the county. This was formally recognised by Her Majesty, Queen Elizabeth II in 1958, and letters patent confirming this were issued in 1974.

Windsor Castle is a favourite home of the Royal Family and the largest inhabited castle in the world. Just across the river is Eton College – the most famous public school in the world. It has educated nineteen British Prime Ministers and sent forth 'a cohort of distinguished figures'. Windsor Great Park is owned by the Crown Estate and comprises 4,800 acres of woodland, farms and open fields, much of which is now open to the public. In former times it used to be part of a huge royal hunting forest, dating back to the mid-thirteenth century.

Not only has the county acquired a royal status, but royal patronage has been bestowed on a number of sporting events within its boundary. Royal Ascot is the world's most famous race meeting and was founded by Queen Anne in 1711. Members of the Royal Family still lead the procession from Windsor Castle to Ascot each day during Royal Ascot week. H.R.H. Prince Albert became Henley Regatta's first Royal Patron in 1851, and since his death, the reigning monarch has always consented to being patron.

The majestic Thames – the second longest river in the UK – forms Berkshire's northern boundary, and has inspired many writers and artists. Jerome K. Jerome's *Three Men in a Boat* describes an epic journey up the Thames from Kingston to Oxford; the Thames at Cookham Dean provided Kenneth Grahame with the setting for his classic riverside tale *The Wind in the Willows*; Sir Stanley Spencer set his wonderful series of New Testament paintings in and around Cookham.

The Routes

Seven of the routes include the Thames Path (between Windsor and Pangbourne) as part of the itinerary. The remaining three are in the eastern corner of the county, south of the M4.

Nine of the routes are either circular, or a figure-of-eight design. One walk is reverse-linear, and requires driving to the end of the walk by car and then travelling to the start by train. That way, the walk can be taken at your own speed and the car will be waiting for you at the finish. All walks range from 5 - 9½ miles and are graded from one to three boots – from easy to the more challenging.

Standard grid references are given for accurate location of starting points using an OS map (or mapping web-sites, such as www.streetmap.co.uk). A postcode or 'nearest postcode' is also given to locate the starting point with the aid of a Sat Nav. If the starting point is not near a postal address, then the 'nearest postcode' may be some distance away from the actual starting point.

The Maps

Although a thorough description of each walk is given and a sketch map provided, it is advisable to take with you a compass (or GPS) and a detailed OS map of the area, should you stray from the route or are forced to cut it short. Conveniently, the whole area is covered by the 159, 160, 171 and 172 OS Explorer maps.

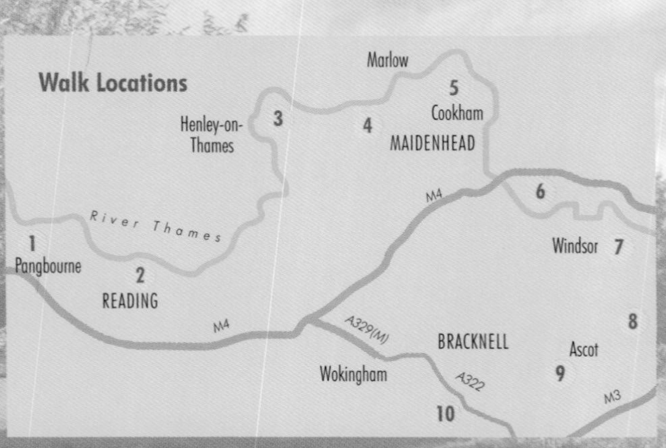

Key to Symbols Used

Level of difficulty:

Easy

Fair

More challenging

Map symbols:

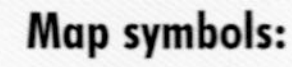

Park & start

Road

Footpath

Railway line

Building / Town

Church

Pub

1 Pangbourne and Purley on Thames

Explore a stretch of the Thames Path that has inspired many writers and artists on this 6½ mile circuit

Jerome K. Jerome's *Three Men in a Boat* is a nineteenth century account of a jaunt up the Thames from Kingston to Oxford. The make-believe mishaps the three friends encounter are laugh-out-loud funny. The humorous anecdotes and benign escapism made the book an instant success when it appeared in 1889. It was at the Swan Inn, behind Pangbourne Weir, that the three friends ended their epic journey and made the return trip to London by train.

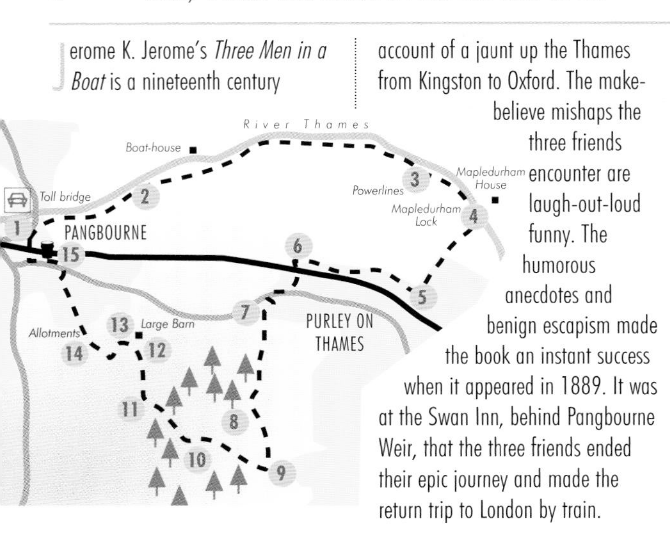

Level:

Length: 6½ miles (10.6 km)

Terrain: Easy walking along Thames Path, through woodland and across field paths

Park and Start: Shoppers short stay car park, Pangbourne (near Working Men's Club).

Start ref: SU 636767

Postcode: RG8 7DA

Public transport: Buses 132, 133 and 142 from Reading Station stop in Pangbourne.

Refreshments and facilities: Teashop at Mapledurham Lock; The Star, Pangbourne; The Swan, Pangbourne.

1 Exit the shoppers car park and then turn left along road. After 50 metres, cross road (before toll bridge) and take unmade track to right of the Dolphin centre. Cut left, at the first opportunity, across water meadow, and when you reach the river, bear right along the Thames Path. Look left for a fine view of the white lattice girder toll bridge across the river. Pass numerous pleasure crafts moored on nearside riverbank, and at end of meadow, cross wooden footbridge into next field. When river swings round to right, cross footbridge and go through metal gate.

2 At end of field, go through wooden swing gate and past small boathouse on opposite river bank. Here there is no path as such – merely indentations along edge of meadow, worn down by numerous feet. And the landscape is very open – with wide uncluttered skies all around. A good place for a picnic, if the weather is fine. Across the river, a wooded escarpment rises majestically, and provides some relief to the flat and featureless landscape, on this side of the Thames. Go through another gate and past a small island in centre of river.

Lattice girder toll bridge across Thames

Boats moored along Pangbourne meadows

Right: *Boat house on Buckinghamshire bank of the Thames*

3 Pass a diminutive pylon and a section of riverbank hedged with blackthorn for 100 metres. Go through two wooden gates into Mapledurham Lock, where the river splits into two channels, with a large weir on one side and a lock for river craft on the other.

4 Pass teashop and continue across wooden footbridge at end of lock. Keep following Thames Path across field and bear left when you reach a lane. Pass several houses, and through an unusual gate that straddles driveway.

5 At the end of the lane, go right along Purley village road. Pass Infant School, and when road swings sharp left, go right along

The African Queen near Mapledurham Lock

Cruiser leaving Mapledurham Lock

Kenneth Grahame, author of The Wind in the Willows, lived in Church Cottage, Pangbourne and Mapledurham House or Hardwick House may have been the inspiration for his 'Toad Hall'.

Mapledurham Lock

bridleway. Follow walled path round to left and keep ahead at next junction. Continue along path, fenced with green railings, parallel to railway cutting, with wonderful views across fields on right.

6 At the end, turn left across railway bridge, and when you reach the main road, go right. Take the first left up Beech Road, and when the road swings left, go right along concealed footpath.

7 Go through kissing gate and then bear sharply left along rising path into spinney. When woodland ends, continue across open field towards next pocket of woodland. Bear left along edge of woodland and follow lightly-trodden path round to the right.

8 At end of field, bear half left (at yellow arrow) along rising track (popular with dog walkers) and across wide open field.

9 Turn obliquely right at next junction to follow dead-straight track downhill. At end of field, bear half-left along path next to broken post and wire fence.

Railway bridge near Purley

10 Go through 'Susie's gate' into woodland and keep ahead at next fingerpost.

11 After a few paces, fork right to follow meandering path through beech woodland. This eventually joins up with a 'recreational trail' along woodland edge, and passes a short section of dark green yew trees.

12 At next junction (waymarked with white arrows), go left out of the woodland and then left again down a farm track, with field on left hand side. Go right at next T-junction along farm track that swings left to join tarred lane near large barn and waterwheel.

13 At next T-junction, go left along road and then right after 100 metres over stile and across field. Go through two gates in quick succession, and across wooden foot-bridge over dried-up river bed.

14 At next signpost, keep ahead through swing gate and follow path across allotments. When houses appear, maintain direction along narrow alleyway. Cross road (near fire station) and keep following alleyway to main road.

15 Turn left here past The Star pub, and after a short distance, cross road at Zebra crossing. Bear right at mini-roundabout (near the George Hotel) and continue under railway bridge. Cross road, and return to short stay car park, where the walk began.

In 2005, the comedians Griff Rhys Jones, Dara O'Briain, and Rory McGrath embarked on a recreation of Jerome K. Jerome's novel, which was to become a regular yearly BBC TV series Three Men in a Boat.

Beech woodland near Pangbourne

2 Reading and Shiplake

A 7 mile reverse-linear walk from Reading to Shiplake Station along the Thames Path

Reading is the county town of Berkshire and is situated at the confluence of two rivers: the Thames and the Kennet. The latter flows through the heart of the Oracle shopping centre and past some of the most historic parts of the town. Reading is also a commercial centre with cutting-edge business parks, two universities and one of England's largest music festivals. Famous celebrities born in Reading include: Mike Oldfield, Chris Tarrant, Kate Winslet and Ricky Gervais – whose recent film *Cemetery Junction* was set in a Reading suburb in 1973.

Level: 🥾🥾

Length: 7 miles (11.3 km)

Terrain: Flat watery ramble along the Thames Path.

Park and Start: Shiplake Station car park (or roadside parking along Station Road). Take a train to Reading Station (changing at Twyford), where the walk starts.

Start ref: SU 776797

Postcode (nearest): RG9 3NY

Public transport: Reading Station

Refreshments and facilities: The Baskerville, Shiplake; The Great House, Sonning; Fisherman's Cottage and the Jolly Angler, Reading.

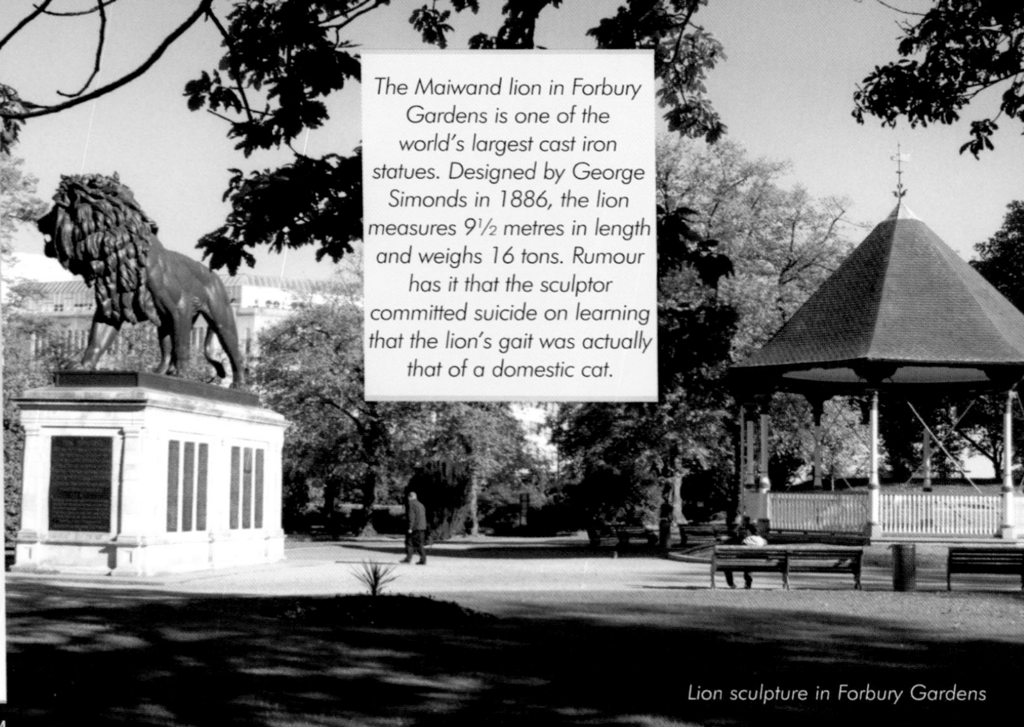

The Maiwand lion in Forbury Gardens is one of the world's largest cast iron statues. Designed by George Simonds in 1886, the lion measures 9½ metres in length and weighs 16 tons. Rumour has it that the sculptor committed suicide on learning that the lion's gait was actually that of a domestic cat.

Lion sculpture in Forbury Gardens

1 Exit Reading Station and then go immediately left past a monument of Edward VII. Keep left at roundabout, past the bus stop for Rail Air and the Apex Plaza. Cross road at Corn Stores and go right at next roundabout. Bear half left across road and make for archway into Forbury Gardens.

2 Continue past the large Lion Statue and bandstand and exit the gardens at Forbury Coffee Bar. Keep ahead through archway, near plaque for Reading Abbey. Follow road round to the left past a large glass-fronted modern office block. When you reach the Kings Road, go right and then immediately left, after the Christian Science Reading Room.

From1785 to 1786 Jane Austen and her sister Cassandra attended the Reading Ladies Boarding School, which was situated within the Old Abbey gateway, near Forbury Gardens.

3 Cross footbridge over the River Kennet (opposite Queens Road car park) and then bear left along footpath. This canal side walk in the heart of the metropolis could be Reading's answer to St Petersburg (minus the Hermitage). Continue under two road bridges and past the Huntley and Palmers building, established in 1841.

Oscar Wilde was imprisoned in Reading Gaol from 1895 until 1897 for 'homosexual offences'. Whilst in exile, he wrote The Ballad of Reading Gaol *about a hanging he witnessed there that profoundly affected him.*

Huntley and Palmers building

4 Smart riverside apartments line the opposite riverbank, before you reach a small island (or eyot) , near the Bel and the Dragon restaurant. Pass the Fisherman's Cottage pub and Blakes Lock. The large imposing structure on the opposite riverbank is the old gasworks and opposite it the Jolly Anglers pub. Pass a school and continue under two railway bridges.

Disused gasworks

Small eyot near Bel and the Dragon

5 The River Kennet now merges with the River Thames and becomes appreciably wider. Continue along Thames Path with a large marina on the opposite riverbank. This section of the towpath is paved and very popular with joggers. When the tarmac runs out, continue along the edge of a water meadow, which business park employees sometimes use as a soccer pitch.

6 Cross bridge into second water meadow, and continue along the Thames Path as it curves round to the right and enters a short section of woodland. Cross footbridge over a backwater and follow towpath as it swings sharply to the left. Pass Reading Blue Coat School Boat Club, and then Sonning Lock soon after.

Sonning Bridge

7 When you reach Sonning Bridge, gain the road and bear left across bridge. Cross road and then go right over footbridge to regain the Thames Path. Continue along narrow footpath past a spinney of tall poplars. Go through hedged section of towpath with fields on left hand side.

8 In due course, the river bends sharply left and rugby pitches come into view. Go through a swing gate into woodland, where the river swings sharply right and the path goes through a swampy area. After another left-handed meander, go through a gate and along the right hand edge of a sports field. Cut diagonally across a rugby pitch, and aim for the white house on the nearby hillside.

9 Cross a wooden footbridge near Shiplake College Boathouse and along the edge of a boat launching area – an ideal place to stop for refreshment. Cross a foot-bridge over a backwater and go through a metal swing gate and past two large maple trees. Continue along

George Orwell (author of Animal Farm *and* 1984*) spent his early childhood in Shiplake and Alfred Lord Tennyson was married at Shiplake church in 1850.*

Narrowboat near Sonning

right hand edge of cattle field with weir on right hand side. Go through two more gates before reaching a way-marked junction.

10 Turn left here towards Shiplake and along the edge of high flint wall. Zig zag right and then left at junction along narrow enclosed path, bounded by large conifer hedge. Go through two more gates and then bear left over a bridge.

11 Turn right along road and continue until you reach a T-junction. Turn right for the station car park or left if you've parked your car along Station Road. If you came by train, then there is a regular service (every 40 minutes) to Reading (changing at Twyford).

Above: *Meadow on outskirts of Shiplake*
Below: *Shiplake Station*

3 Henley-on-Thames

Follow the famous Henley Royal Regatta course on this 5 mile circuit along the Thames Path

Henley Regatta was inaugurated in 1839, and Prince Albert became its first Royal Patron in 1851. Since then the reigning monarch has always consented to being patron of the event. Unlike most rowing events, Henley operates a knock-out draw with only two boats in each heat. This can involve up to 90 races per day comprising of Eights, Fours, Coxless Pairs and Double Sculls. The length of the course is 1 mile and 550 yards – 112 metres longer than the standard international distance of 2000 metres.

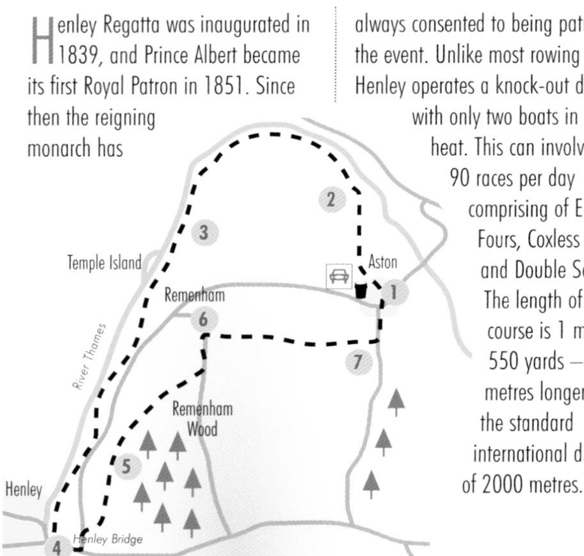

Level:
Length: 5 miles (8 km)
Terrain: Fairly flat ramble along Thames Path, through woodland and across field paths.
Park and Start: The Flower Pot pub car park in Aston (patrons only).
Alternative start: Park in Henley and proceed to Henley Bridge. Pick up walk from point 4.
Start ref: SU 784842
Postcode: RG9 3DG
Public transport: Henley Station is around 500 metres away from point 4.
Refreshments and facilities: The Flower Pot, Aston; pubs in Henley.

Cruiser on the Thames near Hambleden Weir

1 Walk past The Flower Pot pub down Aston Ferry Lane, and take the first left along a hedged path. Go right at T-junction to join a wide gravel drive across water meadows. Apart from the occasional tree, there is nothing to block the view across this wide uncluttered landscape – Henley's answer to the fens. Patches of red poppies bloom here during the summer months. Cross over a small stream, and then turn left to join the Thames Path.

Coxed eights warming up for Henley Regatta

2 Pass the 300 metre footway over the weir to Hambleden Mill, and keep ahead along the Thames Path. The path curves gently to the left to follow the meandering river. If you come during Henley Regatta week (recommended), the river will be a hive of activity: from grand luxury cruisers, pleasure boats ferrying sight-seers, to eight man rowing crews limbering up for the big event.

Coxless pairs

Temple Island is situated a mile and a half downstream of Henley and marks the start of the Henley Royal Regatta course. The Temple itself is a folly, conceived by James Wyatt as a fishing lodge for Fawley Court – the mansion on the Henley Reach, designed by Sir Christopher Wren.

Starting point for Henley Regatta course

Punting on the Thames

3 In due course, you will pass Temple Island, and the reach of the Thames which marks the start of 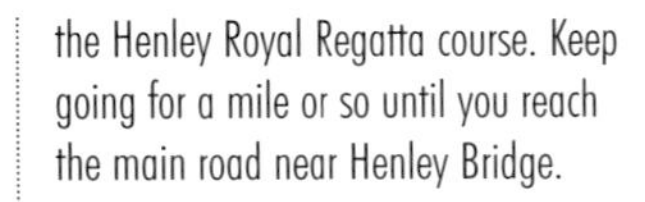 the Henley Royal Regatta course. Keep going for a mile or so until you reach the main road near Henley Bridge.

The River and Rowing Museum in Henley hosts a permanent exhibition of Kenneth Grahame's classic riverside tale The Wind in the Willows.

Travelling in style

4 Go right to visit Henley town centre, or left to continue the walk. Turn left at the Little Angel pub, along Remenham Road. Two hundred metres after a left hand bend, bear right through a swing gate and along a gravel track. Cross stile and then cut diagonally left across a small golf course. Go up slope, and over stile into woodland.

The first Oxford and Cambridge boat race took place at Henley-on-Thames in 1829 and newspapers reported that 20,000 spectators came to watch.

Little Angel pub, Henley

5 When you emerge from the tree cover, go half right across slope of meadow and over stile into the darkness of Remenham Wood. Continue along a rising path, flanked by saplings, which eventually levels out and starts descending. When the wood ends, maintain direction on a rising path across large corn field to crest of hill. Look left for good views of the Thames Path. Aim for solitary oak and when you reach a road, go left.

6 Before you reach woodland, go right over a stile and along a wide gravel farm track between large fields. Keep going for ca. 600 metres and when track veers right, keep ahead along smaller path. Look left for grand views across water meadows. Pass large hedge made from holly and laurel and when you reach a junction, keep ahead through swing gate and along left hand edge of field.

7 Climb stile and maintain direction along field edge to road (Aston Ferry Lane). Bear left here and keep going until you reach the car park of the Flower Pot pub.

Farm track leading to Aston

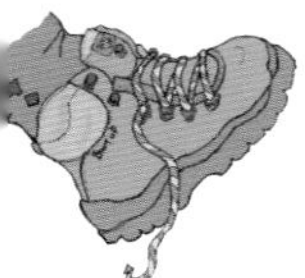

4 Hurley and Marlow

A fashionable riverside town and a nineteenth century suspension bridge are both on offer on this 5½ mile figure-of-eight walk along the Thames Path.

The River Thames made Marlow what it is today, putting it on the map first as a river crossing and then as an inland port. One of the town's outstanding features is the elegant nineteenth century suspension bridge – the work of William Tierney Clark in 1832, who also designed Hammersmith Bridge and the bridge across the Danube at Budapest. Marlow's emergence as a fashionable riverside resort has attracted a host of famous names to the town, including the poet Shelley, Jerome K. Jerome and T.S. Eliot.

Level:
Length: 5½ miles (8.8 km)
Terrain: Easy walking along Thames Path, through woodland and across field paths.
Park and Start: Hurley village car park, opposite church (free).
Start ref: SU 826840
Postcode (nearest): SL6 5NB
Public transport: Bus 239 from Henley to Maidenhead stops in Hurley.
Refreshments and facilities: Ye Olde Bell, Hurley; Hurley café; pubs and cafés in Marlow.

1 From the entrance to the Hurley village car park, bear left and follow the public footpath to the river. Pass opulent mansions on the left and continue to a wooden footbridge. Cross it and bear right along the Thames Path. Continue past Hurley Lock and teashop and onto Hurley Lock Island, where the Thames has split into several channels and created this unusual river island.

Cross another wooden footbridge to the Berkshire bank

Hurley Lock Island was described by Jerome K. Jerome as a place: 'I could stay a month without having sufficient time to drink in all the beauty of the scene'.

Boats moored at Hurley Lock Island

of the Thames and bear left through clump of trees to join wide gravel drive. Cross section of parkland and then pass through gate into woodland. Note the vast array of boats moored on the opposite riverbank.

3 Cross the river again, via the Temple footbridge – an impressive looking structure, built in 1989 to replace the old ferry. Continue along the Buckinghamshire bank of the Thames past Temple Lock

The Thames near Hurley

Narrowboat at Hurley Lock Island

and weir. Here the footpath becomes tarred for a while, but then reverts back to a wide grassy walkway, with pastoral landscape to the left of path.

4 Continue past the fourteenth century Bisham Abbey – now the Sports Council's training centre and sailing club – and Bisham's twelfth century church, which graces the opposite riverbank. It won't be long before the spire of All Saints' church and Marlow's famous nineteenth century suspension bridge comes into view.

5 Pass Higginson Park on the left, where a statue of Marlow's Olympic rowing hero, Sir Steve Redgrave is located. Just before the suspension bridge bear left away from the river along a paved path.

Bisham church

Bisham Abbey is one of the UK's five National Sports Centres, which provides elite athletes with a range of specialist facilities, expertise and residential accommodation, suitable for world class sporting talent.

Keep going until you reach a mini roundabout, and then turn left along Pound Lane. Pass Court Garden car park on left and maintain direction along road.

Bronze statue of Sir Steve Redgrave

A bronze statue of the Olympic rower Sir Steve Redgrave is situated in Higginson Park, Marlow. After striking gold at the Sydney Olympics in 2000, he became Britain's only athlete ever to have won gold at five consecutive Olympic Games.

Narrowboat moored at Marlow

6 After a few hundred metres, bear left along a public byway (Lower Pound Lane) and keep ahead when the byway merges with a private road. Ignore the next footpath left and continue along metalled lane. Cross bridge over stream, and when tarmac runs out (at Pens Place), keep ahead along footpath, with avenue of laurel bushes on left.

The poet Shelley and his wife Mary lived at 104 West Street, Marlow, and it was here that he wrote his longest poem The Revolt of Islam, *and his wife completed her Gothic masterpiece* Frankenstein.

7 Go through kissing gate with sign saying 'Quarry farms, footpath only'. Walk along edge of

Marlow Town Regatta and Festival takes place in Higginson Park in mid June and features competitive rowing on the river with all the traditional ambience of a classic regatta.

Feeding the swans at Marlow

Marlow suspension bridge

corn field with the Thames Path, one field away to your left.

8 When you reach a T-junction, go left along tarmac drive and towards the river.

9 When you reach the Thames Path, bear right and retrace your steps, past Temple Lock and across the Temple footbridge.

10 Half way along wooded section, turn left at signpost, away from the Thames, and along fenced footpath. Go through kissing gate and then bear right along gravel track between fields. Pass caravan park on right, and maintain direction at next signpost.

11 Cross cattle grid and when drive bears sharp right, go left along public footpath. Pass paddocks on right and continue along narrow fenced alleyway and through metal kissing gate to a road, with Ye Olde Bell pub on left.

12 Cross road and bear right along paved footpath. Keep ahead at junction, and continue past Hurley old farm shop and tithe barn to the village car park.

Temple footbridge

5 Cookham

Follow in an artist's footsteps on this exhilarating 9½ mile figure-of-eight walk in and around Cookham

To the painter Stanley Spencer, Cookham was an earthly paradise – a 'village in heaven'. He endowed it with a numinous quality and was aware, from an early age, of the rich religious significance of the place. The village formed a leitmotif throughout his work and provided a setting for many of his New Testament paintings. At Cookham, 'The Word became flesh' – quite literally – 'and moved into the neighbourhood'. The artist could often be seen, trundling his painting gear around the village in an old pram.

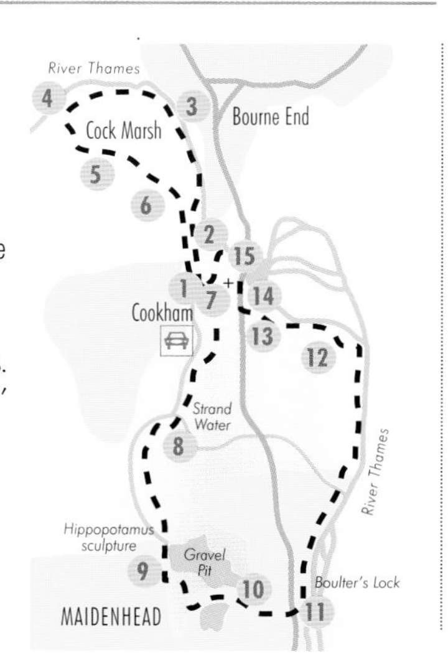

Level:

Length: 9½ miles (15.4km)

Terrain: Remarkably varied walk along Thames Path, across fields and urban fringe.

Park and Start: Cookham Moor car park.

Start ref: SU 894854

Postcode (nearest): SL6 9SB

Public transport: Arriva bus 37 from Maidenhead to High Wycombe stops in Cookham.

Refreshments and facilities: The Bounty Café; Pubs in Cookham: The Crown; The Kings Head; Bel and the Dragon.

1 With your back to the car park entrance, proceed in the opposite direction, towards a public footpath fingerpost. Go through a swing gate and across a wide expanse of grassland (Marsh Meadow), which doubles as a dog walking corridor. To your right, the masts of sailing dinghies from Cookham Sailing Club herald the approach of Old Father Thames.

2 Maintain direction when you reach the Thames Path, and keep walking until you reach a metal kissing gate (near a bench). Proceed into Cock Marsh (N.T. land) and along an avenue of willows, with the Thames to your right, and some impressive mansions and cruisers, on the opposite riverbank.

Railway bridge over the Thames at Cookham

3 Proceed under a railway bridge, through a swing gate, and along the riverbank with bungalows to your left. Pass The Bounty Café, and when the bungalows end, continue through swing gate and across a field, passing a small beach near the water's edge. This is where the crowds start to thin and the dog walkers are all walked out. Go through another swing gate (with a makeshift return mechanism) and continue to Ferry Cottage, where the gravel track bears left away from the river.

4 Keep ahead after a hundred metres, and proceed to a waymarked junction. Go left here along a wide grassy strip, until you

Steep chalk hillside overlooking Cock Marsh

reach a signpost and a swing gate. Go though it into an area of chalk grassland. When you reach the foot of a hill, go half left up a steep slope. As you gain height, you are treated to fabulous panoramic views of Cock Marsh, the sweeping arc of the River Thames, and the hills and villages beyond it. This is an excellent spot to stop and savour the view.

5 When you reach a junction near the top, go left along a narrow well-worn path. At the next fork, take the path that contours round the hill, through bushes and shrubbery. The undulating path descends gradually at first, then goes through a sharp horse-shoe bend before dropping down to a junction. Go right through a swing gate and under a railway arch.

6 Bear right here to follow the yellow waymark, along edge of golf course. At the earliest opportunity, drop down to a sunken lane that runs parallel to the edge of the course. When you reach a fingerpost, maintain direction over footbridge, with ditch on left hand side. Pass a small pond on left and continue until you reach the car park where the walk began. Maintain direction over Cookham Moor and towards the Crown Pub. When you reach the main road, go straight across towards the war memorial and along School Lane.

7 Bear right after 50 metres towards Moor Hall (now the Chartered Institute of Marketing). Go left before hall, along narrow enclosed

Cornfield near Strand Water

path (Green Way East) with wall of building on right hand side. Pass school playing fields on left and fields on right, before reaching a clump of Scots pines, where the path veers half right. At the next junction, keep ahead along Green Way East. To the right, you'll notice a narrow channel of water, sequestered by trees, known as Strand Water.

8 At the end of the field, go right at the finger post, and over a footbridge. Cross another footbridge and then bear left at next fingerpost along field path (Green Way West). Follow this wide walkway to a junction, then bear half left along a wide gravel path. Ignore next left turn (30 metres later) and keep ahead at next junction near quarry, along permissive cycleway.

Hippopotamus sculpture

Maintain direction at junction and re-join cycleway after short distance. Eventually path swings to the left, and leads to a bridge, with an unusual hip-popotamus sculpture nearby.

9 Go left here along permitted cycleway, keeping boundary fence of gravel pits on left. When you reach a sign saying: 'Caution walkers. Use passing places', bear right along permissive cycleway. At end of field, go left along footpath and through swing gate to join Summer Leaze Road.

10 At end of road, go half right along narrow enclosed foot-path. Turn left along road and keep going until you reach the main road (Ray Mead Road).

11 Cross it, then turn left past Boulter's Lock to join the Thames path. Keep following the river

In the late nineteenth century Boulter's Lock was one of the busiest and most popular locks on the Thames. The grand reach from here to Cookham is described in Three Men in a Boat *as 'perhaps the sweetest stretch of all the river'.*

Rivercraft on the Thames along Cliveden Reach

for 2.5 Km, past opulent mansions, and through a wooded section, until the path eventually veers left away from the river and into woodland. Cross a driveway and continue along hedged path to a lane.

12 Turn left along tarred lane,

Stanley Spencer looked upon Cookham High Street as the nave of a church and made it the setting for many of his paintings. The house where he was born, Fernlea, is marked with a blue plaque.

which is signed 'The Thames Path' (even though there is no footpath and you left the River Thames some time ago). Eventually houses appear and the lane veers left to meet the main road.

13 Cross road and bear right towards the Stanley Spencer Gallery. Maintain direction at junction and take the next left at sign for the eleventh century church.

14 Continue through churchyard and past Holy Trinity church, Cookham. Maintain direction and when you reach the River Thames, bear left along Bell Rope Meadow.

15 Take the first left at fingerpost and at end of drive, go half right through two swing gates. Continue along narrow avenue with low wall on right hand side. At the end, bear right across Cookham Moor to return to car park where the walk began.

Holy Trinity churchyard was the setting for one of Spencer's most important works, The Resurrection, Cookham. *The church itself contains a reproduction of his most well-known religious painting,* The Last Supper.

Holy Trinity church, Cookham

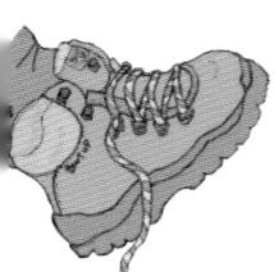

6 Dorney and Bray

A 6 mile ramble along the edge of a world-class rowing lake selected for the 2012 Olympics

Dorney Lake is a world-class rowing and flat-water canoeing centre and has been selected to host the kayak and rowing events in the 2012 Olympic and Paralympic Games. The lake was the venue for the World Rowing Championships in 2006, and gained high praise from spectators and competitors alike.The 2.2 km, eight-lane course, was constructed to international standards by Eton College in 2006, and the Eton College Boat Club use it as their training venue all year round.

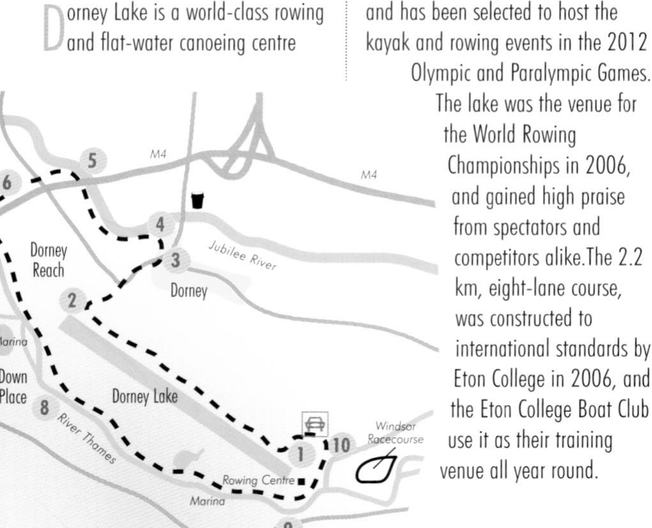

Level:

Length: 6 miles (9.7 km)

Terrain: Fairly flat watery ramble along rowing channel, the Jubilee River and the Thames Path.

Park and Start: Free car park at Boveney, provided by Eton College.

Start ref: SU 939777

Postcode (nearest): SL4 6QQ

Public transport: Redline buses 63 and 68 from Slough to Maidenhead stop in Dorney.

Refreshments and facilities: The Pineapple, Dorney.

1 Proceed to car park entrance and then bear left along road. At first right hand bend, go left along public footpath. Cross cattle grid and proceed along tarmac drive and over grassy sward to Dorney Lake – Eton College's 2.2 km rowing channel. Bear right and walk along footpath beside rowing channel. The distance is clearly defined with white markers every 250 metres. This is rather a civilized way to start the walk with wide uncluttered skies all around. A profusion of walkers, joggers and cyclists frequent the public access routes around the lake.

2 About 100 metres before the end, bear 90 degrees right away from channel and over a grassy bank. Aim for the triangular 'Give Way' sign and continue along tarmac drive, with Arboretum car park on left. Proceed along avenue lined with horse chestnut trees and maintain direction when you reach a road (Court Lane). Follow footpath and cycleway past St James's churchyard and the entrance to Dorney Court.

Rowers on Dorney Lake

Dorney means 'island of bees' and the locally produced honey is renowned for its delicate, light flavours. The first pineapple in England was grown at Dorney Court and presented to Charles II in 1661.

Before you reach the main road, go left over stile and

Bridge over the Jubilee River

along fenced path. Proceed through gate and then bear left (near wooden footbridge) along gravel track, beside the Jubilee River.

4 Continue along track which swings to the right as it follows direction of river. Keep ahead at next fingerpost along National Cycle Network 61 and under the M4 motorway bridge.

5 Take the next left along public footpath bounded by large conifer hedge. Join driveway when path ends and then bear half left along rising path into woodland. When you reach a road (near the motorway bridge) cross it at the appropriate point, and continue down meandering walkway to another road. Maintain direction and at next road

Celebrity chef, Heston Blumenthal, has developed a scientific approach to cooking, and his restaurant in Bray (the Fat Duck) has won 3 Michelin stars and was voted Best Restaurant in the World in 2005.

junction, bear half left along footpath.

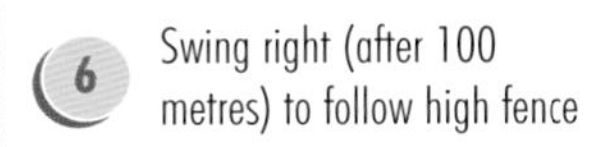

6 Swing right (after 100 metres) to follow high fence

Millennium signpost (National Cycle Network)

bordering M4. The sound can be deafening at times, but you only need endure it for a little while. At the next bridge, descend staircase to the Thames Path and bear left along it.

7 Continue past impressive looking gardens, Monkey Island Hotel, Bray Marina and an unusual signpost for the National Cycle Network.

8 Pass Down Place (with its distinctive clock tower and cupola), Oakley Court Hotel, Windsor Marina, and the Eton Excelsior rowing club. When a mobile home park

Cruiser near Windsor Marina

Oakley Court Hotel has been used in various Hammer Horror movie productions, including The Curse of Frankenstein *(1957) and* The Rocky Horror Picture Show *(1975).*

Woodland near Thames Path

appears on the opposite riverbank, the brick-red bridges of Dorney Lake should also come into view.

9 The river then veers sharp left and in due course passes Eton College boat house.

10 When you see the white railings of Windsor Racecourse on the opposite riverbank, take the next left away from the river and towards a disused church (St Mary Magdalen, Boveny). Follow path to left of church and after 200 metres go left through gate and into car park where the walk began.

7 Windsor and Eton

A 5½ mile circuit along the Thames Path, taking in Royal Windsor and Eton College

Windsor Castle is a favorite home of the Royal Family, and the largest inhabited castle in the world. The site was chosen by William the Conqueror, but the oldest parts of the castle, including the round tower, were built in the reign of Henry II. The Upper Ward contains the State Apartments as well as the Sovereign's Private Apartments. The Lower Ward is dominated by St George's Chapel, which for 500 years has been home of the college of St George and the Order of the Garter. The chapel has been described as 'one of the supreme achievements of English Perpendicular Gothic design'. Ten former monarchs have been buried there, including King George VI and the Queen Mother.

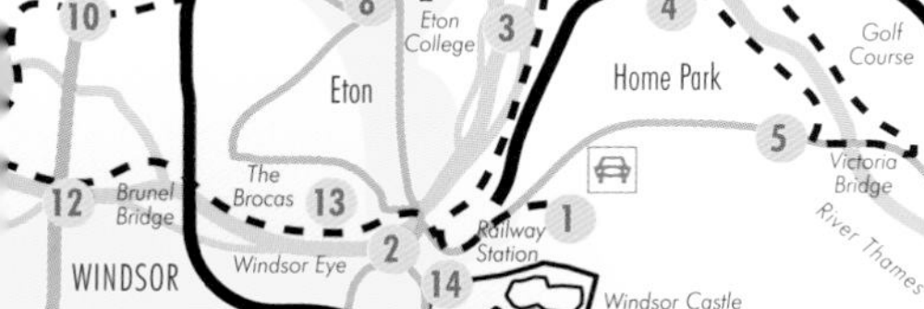

Level:
Length: 5½ miles (8.7 km)
Terrain: Fairly flat walking along the Thames Path and nearby water meadows.
Park and Start: King Edward VII car park, Windsor (pay and display).
Start ref: SU 971774
Postcode (nearest): SL4 1QF
Public transport: Bus 71 from Heathrow Airport (Terminal 5) stops in Windsor.
Refreshments and facilities: Pubs in Windsor and Eton.

1 Exit the Edward VII car park, cross the busy B470 and then bear left in the direction of Windsor town centre. After passing Windsor & Eton Riverside Station and the Bel and the Dragon restaurant, turn right along a pedestrianized walkway (Thames Street).

2 Just before the bridge linking Windsor and Eton, turn right along the Thames Path. Pass commercial buildings, the River House restaurant and continue along the edge of a car park. The Thames Path soon becomes a roadway, with a railway line alongside it.

3 When you reach a boat-yard, bear half left and then right through a kissing gate, and along the

Above: *Bridge across the Thames linking Windsor and Eton*
Below: *Cruiser on the Thames near Windsor Bridge*

French Brothers boat cruise

Thames Path. The route continues across a water meadow and then swings right under a railway viaduct.

4 Pass information board for Home Park, with playing fields and rugby pitches on right and good views of Windsor Castle beyond them.

The Home Park – an extensive area of playing fields, pitches and tennis courts – dates back to the late 1600s when the first work was undertaken to construct a great garden on the land between Windsor Castle, the river, and Datchet.

The Victoria Bridge was built in 1851, paid for partly by the Windsor, Staines and Richmond Railway Company who were keen to have access to Windsor across part of the castle property. Prince Albert is said to have had a hand in its design and the original bridge was built of cast iron with stone abuttments.

Black Potts Weir

5 Just before you reach another bridge, go right across greensward and up bank to gain the road. Bear left along footway over Victoria Bridge (built in 1851). Take the next left after bridge, down concrete steps in hedge and then left past a triple bunker along edge of Datchet Golf Course. When the track peters out, maintain direction until you reach the Thames Path. Continue past Black Potts Weir and under a railway viaduct.

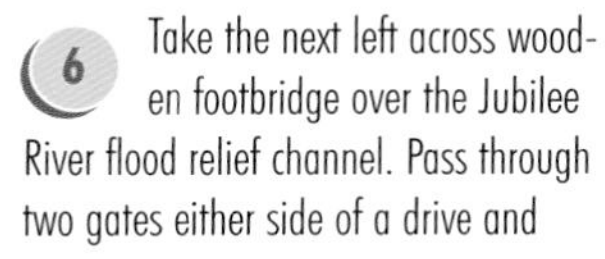

6 Take the next left across wooden footbridge over the Jubilee River flood relief channel. Pass through two gates either side of a drive and

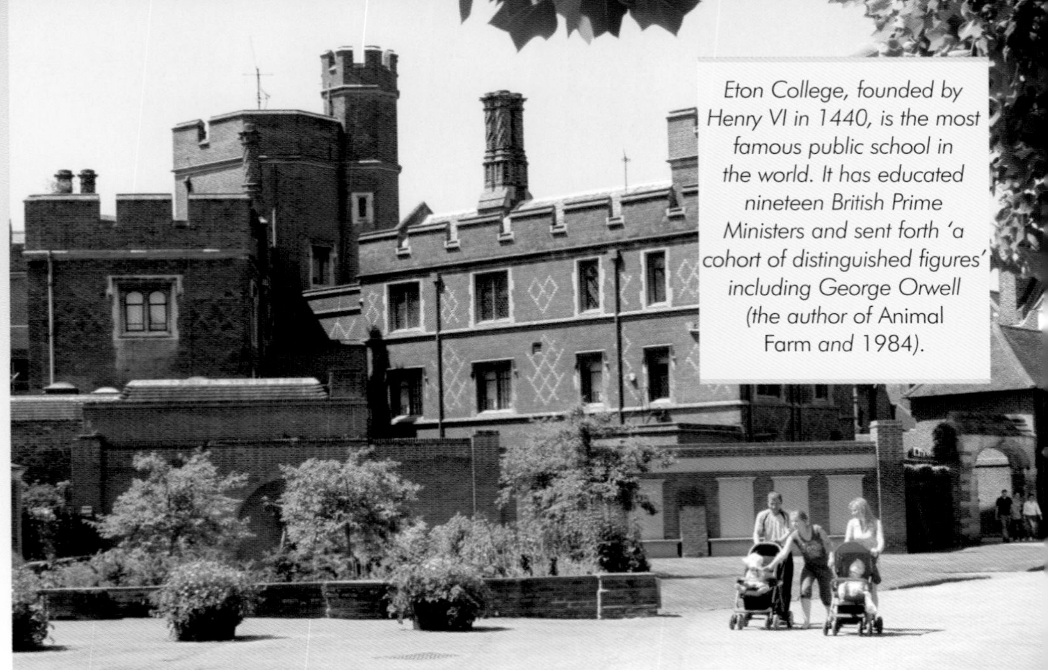

Eton College, founded by Henry VI in 1440, is the most famous public school in the world. It has educated nineteen British Prime Ministers and sent forth 'a cohort of distinguished figures' including George Orwell (the author of Animal Farm *and* 1984*).*

Eton College from the playing fields

across waste ground. Go through a metal kissing gate and past two boat houses. When you reach a road, bear left along it for about 100 metres.

7 Turn left across metal foot-bridge that leads to the Eton College Playing Fields. Keep going along a gravel path flanked with lime trees. Cross bridge over stream and maintain direction towards Eton College buildings. To the left lies Windsor Castle (the seat of Monarchy) and up ahead Eton College (the seat of Learning) and the most famous public school in England. Swing right when the track ends and then left through an archway and across a courtyard, to pass the main college buildings, with their fluted chimneys, castle-shaped turrets and flying buttresses.

8 When you emerge at a main road, go straight across, and keep to the right of the college library with its dome-shaped roof. Continue up Common Lane, passing the Hop Garden and tenements from a difference social era, with the 'Tradesmen's Entrance' clearly designated. As the buildings get sparser and fields start to appear, bear half-left up the first public footpath. Keep to left hand edge of meadow, and when you reach a well-worn path, bear half-right along it.

9 Cross road and maintain direction along tarred walk-way towards Eton Wick,with allotments on right. After 200 metres, go right under railway viaduct and continue towards dual carriageway.

View of Windsor Castle from The Brocas

10 Take the path that burrows under the dual carriageway (A322), and note the 'pop-art' graffiti on the walls of the tunnel and the adjoining four arches. Keep going across the meadow and bear left at the next junction.

11 When you reach the Thames Path, bear left along it. Cross footbridge and keep following the river as it meanders right and then left past Royal Windsor Racecourse.

12 Pass under the A322 again, cross bridge over backwater, and pass beneath Brunel's railway bridge. The Windsor Eye should now loom large on the opposite riverbank.

Tourists on Windsor boat cruise

13 Maintain direction across The Brocas with fabulous views of Windsor Castle's round tower across the river. Join a tarmac road that leads you past the Waterman's Arms and Eton College Boathouse. When you reach Eton High Street, turn right over the Victorian bridge that spans the River Thames and leads to pedestrianized walkway (Thames Street).

14 When you reach the end, keep ahead if you wish to explore the Windsor shops and Castle. To continue the walk turn left and retrace your steps to the King Edward VII car park.

8 Windsor Great Park

A 5¾ mile circuit across royal parkland, taking in the polo grounds and The Valley Gardens

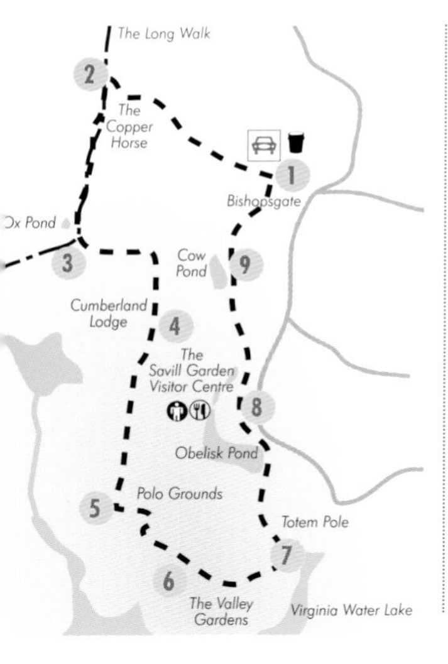

Windsor Great Park is owned by the Crown Estate and comprises 4,800 acres of woodland, farms and open fields, much of which is now open to the public. In former times it used to be part of a huge royal hunting forest, dating back to the mid-thirteenth century. A 3 mile long avenue of trees – the Long Walk – links Windsor Castle with the Copper Horse, an equestrian statue of King George III, erected in 1831. Contained within the park are some major visitor attractions including: Virginia Water, the Savill Garden, the Valley Gardens and the polo grounds.

Level: 🥾🥾
Length: 5¾ miles (9.2 km)
Terrain: Relatively flat ramble across royal parkland.
Park and Start: Roadside parking near Bishopsgate, next to Fox and Hounds pub.
Start ref: SU 979722
Postcode: TW20 0XU
Public transport: The number 71 bus from Heathrow (terminal 5) to Windsor via Egham stops at Englefield Green.
Refreshments and facilities: The Fox and Hounds pub, Englefield Green; The Savill Garden Visitor Centre.

The Long Walk to Windsor Castle

1 From the parking area near the Fox and Hounds pub, enter Windsor Great Park via Bishopsgate and proceed along tarmac road towards a pink building. Turn right at road junction and enter Deer Park via the green metal kissing gate. Maintain direction along a wide tarmac road in the direction of Snow Hill, through a vast and magnificent expanse of parkland. Windsor Castle can be glimpsed through the trees to your right and, not far above it, jets coming into land at Heathrow. Cross a grand bridge over a dried-up stream, and when you reach 'The Long Walk' that leads to Windsor Castle, bear left on a rising path towards 'the Copper Horse'.

Savour the fabulous views from Snow Hill of the royal

The Copper Horse

The Copper Horse is an equestrian statue of King George III on Snow Hill, marking the end of the Long Walk from Windsor Castle. The statue depicts the king as an emperor in the roman tradition, riding without stirrups, and was commissioned by his son George IV.

residence, Windsor Castle, the Windsor Eye, and the glint of reservoirs that surround Heathrow. You might even see crows nestling under the cloak of George III. Maintain direction along 'Three Castles Path' and across a sandy horse ride. Exit Deer Park via a metal kissing gate and proceed along a wide enclosed walkway that resembles a racecourse.

Horse riders near Chaplain's Lodge

3 Pass Ox Pond and then bear left at the junction, near Chaplain's Lodge. Cross a horse ride and when you reach a T-junction, bear 90 degrees right (ignoring the first turn to Cumberland Lodge). Keep going along this wide tarmac road, ideal for cycling. The parkland is so neatly manicured, that it must take a whole army of Crown Estate workers to keep it in this pristine condition. On occasions, it can seem too perfect, and a little sterile, as a consequence. Certain sections of the Park are so sparsely populated, that you can sometimes have the whole area to yourself. Other sections – around Virginia Water – are best avoided at peak periods.

Keep going until you reach Cumberland Gate and the start of the polo grounds. Keep ahead for about 800 metres with the polo fields on your left hand side.

At the next junction, bear left in the direction of the Guards Polo

Topiary of equestrian fi at the Guards Polo

Polo match in progress

The Guards Polo Club, was founded in 1953 with HRH Prince Phillip, Duke of Edinburgh, as president and is set in the outstanding natural surroundings of Smith's Lawn. There are around 160 playing members, among whom are some of the highest rated players in the world.

Club. When you reach the club house, turn sharp right towards an information board for Valley Gardens. After a 100 metres, bear left through a gate into the Heather Garden, and keep on the gravel path that winds its way through heather beds and large conifers.

6 Go through a gate to exit Heather Garden, then bear right past a picnic area. To visit the Punchbowl (recommended) - with its spectacular display of azaleas and rhododendrons in spring – follow the signs off to the right. To continue the

Spring azaleas in the Valley Gardens

The Totem Pole near Virginia Water lake

The Totem Pole was a gift from the people of Canada to HM Queen Elizabeth II in June 1958. Standing 100 feet high – one foot for every year – it marks the centenary of British Columbia, which was proclaimed a Crown Colony by Queen Victoria in November 1858.

walk, return to the main track and follow signs for the Totem Pole.

7 Bear left at the Totem Pole in the direction of Savill Garden and Wick Road. Follow the tarmac road on a rising path that swings left and then right. When you reach a junction, go straight across in the direction of Savill Garden. Continue along the right hand edge of Obelisk Pond, and past the Duke of Cumberland's Obelisk and along the edge of Savill Garden car park.

8 Pass in front of Savill Garden Visitor Centre and follow signs for Bishopsgate and Cow Pond. Continue along tarmac road flanked on both sides with rhododendron bushes. When road bears left, keep ahead along untarred lane.

9 Pass a beautiful lily pond (Cow Pond), on the left, and when the avenue ends, bear right to return to Bishopsgate and the Fox and Hounds pub.

Cow Pond covered in water lilies

9 Ascot Heath

Follow the Three Castles Path across the most prestigious racecourse in the country on this delightfully varied 7½ mile circuit

There are few sporting venues that can match the prestige and heritage of the Ascot Racecourse, which was inaugurated in 1811 by Queen Anne. For 200 years, Royal Ascot week has established itself as a national institution and the centrepiece of the British social calendar. Tradition, pageantry and style all meet in a glorious setting at one of the most magnificant racecourses in the country. Each day of Royal Ascot, the reigning monarch and various members of the Royal Family, arrive in horse-drawn carriages with the Royal Procession taking place at the start of each race day.

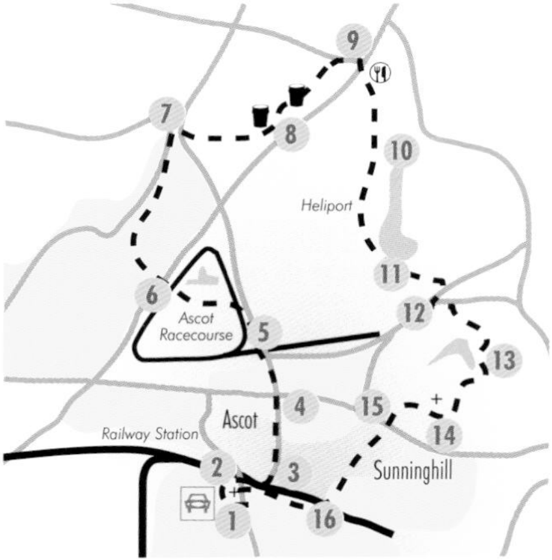

Level:
Length: 7½ miles (12 km)
Terrain: Delightfully varied walk across Ascot Heath, along field paths, through woodland and urban fringe. A fair degree of road walking involved.
Park and Start: Parking area near recreation ground off Victoria Road, South Ascot.
Start ref: SU 924679
Postcode (nearest): SL5 9DS
Public transport: Ascot Station
Refreshments and facilities: Duke of Edinburgh and Rose and Crown pub, Wood End.

1 From the parking area, go left along All Souls Road, and follow it round to the right past All Soul's church.

2 Bear right at the T-junction along Lyndhurst Road, and when you reach the main road turn right. Take the next left along Oliver Road and left again soon afterwards under a railway viaduct.

3 Follow this byway across a pleasant patch of woodland – a wildlife oasis in the midst of urban fringe. When the track splits, keep ahead along a narrow rising path (displaying a 5′ 3″ road sign), to reach a tarred lane. Maintain direction along St George's Lane until you reach the main road (A329).

All Soul's church, Ascot

4 Go left and then right along Winkfield Road. Pass New Mile Road and then go immediately half right up steps to cross the old straight mile racecourse, via the white gates. You may be held up here, if racing is in progress. Maintain direction along tarmac path, with road to your left on a lower level.

5 Descend some steps and then bear left through (a carefully concealed) underpass. Keep ahead along rising path towards Ascot

Main Grandstand, Ascot Racecourse

The Three Castles Path is a 60 mile long distance footpath from Winchester to Windsor Castle which crosses Ascot Heath and provides public access even on race days.

Racing in progress at Royal Ascot

Heath. Follow drive as it swings right and then left across Ascot Heath, with main grandstand on your left. Go right at T-junction and keep following tarmac drive until you exit the race-course via a gate.

6 Cross the busy Windsor Road and keep ahead along Kennel Avenue with its stately lines of Wellingtonia. At the end, go right along Burleigh Avenue, and past a red post box. Keep ahead when larger road joins from the left.

7 After 1 km of linear walking, turn right along main road. Pass Stable House, then bear left through wooden kissing gate (with tri-angular footpath sign). Keep to left hand edge of horse paddocks and

Horse paddocks near Wood End

through three more gates. At end of fourth field, go left through kissing gate into adjoining field and maintain direction. Cross stile and continue along narrow enclosed path. Go through swing gate and follow path as it snakes right and then left. Continue along Kiln Lane, past house with unusual 'birds of prey' sculptures and then a line of bungalows.

8 Turn left past the Duke of Edinburgh pub, and then right past the Rose and Crown. Go right when you reach the main road, and right again (before the Loch Fyne restaurant) along track near Bluebell House.

9 Cross main road and pick up public footpath near Woodend cottages. Keep ahead over woodland ride into a beautifully tranquil pine

Meadow linking Crown Estate woo

and broad leaf woodland, owned by the Crown Estate. Continue along woodland ride as it swings right and then left.

10 Pass two unusual looking stiles with chains on, before crossing a meadow with splendid views. Continue along tarmac drive,

Each day of Royal Ascot, the reigning monarch and members of the Royal Family travel through Windsor Great Park in horse drawn carriages. The route passes along Watersplash Lane and Cheapside Road before joining the race course via a private entrance along the Old Straight Mile course.

with signs warning you not to climb on timber stacks, Pass a heliport on right used to transport the great and the good to Royal Ascot.

11 When you reach a junction (with the Great Pond on left), keep ahead into woodland. Cross foot-bridge, and bear right at the road.

12 At next junction with thatched cottage, turn left along Cheapside Road at the junction with Watersplash Lane. After 100 metres, go right through a wooden swing gate and along an enclosed path with holly hedge on right hand side. Pass recreation area and follow fenced path as it swings to the left, narrows and begins to descend, passing a house and a footbridge.

13 When you reach a T-junction, bear right, along fenced path, and past an expanse of water. After swinging right, path emerges from woodland and becomes a grassy walkway. Go through metal swing gate, past a cemetery and follow wall of St Michael's church round to right and through a parking area.

14 Keep ahead through a gate to follow enclosed walkway, which soon becomes wooded. Take the first left along a narrow enclosed path that leads in due course to a main road. Turn right and then immediately left across busy main road to Coombe Lane.

St Michael and All Angels, Sunninghill

15 Continue along unmade road, passing houses on left hand side. At the next T-junction go right to pass under railway arch.

16 Turn immediately right along tarred footpath, with railway embankment on your right hand side. When footpath ends, maintain direction and continue to the end of Oliver Road. Cross main road and then bear left past parade of shops. Take the next right along Victoria Road to the parking area where the walk began.

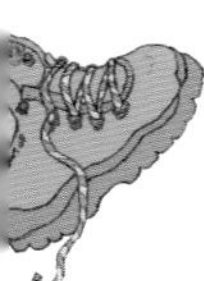

10 Swinley Forest

A 6 mile circuit along woodland rides and forest tracks on the outskirts of Bracknell

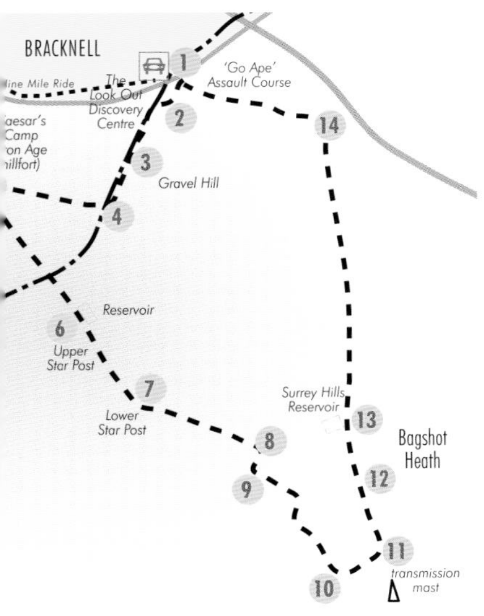

Swinley Forest comprises over 2,600 acres of mainly Scots pine woodland and is owned and managed by the Windsor Crown Estate. It covers an area from Bracknell to Bagshot to the west of the A322. Because of its proximity to Heathrow and the M4 corridor, Bracknell town has attracted many high technology industries including Siemens, Panasonic, Fujitsu, Hewlett Packard, Dell and Boehringer Ingelheim.

Level:
Length: 6 miles (9.8 km)
Terrain: Woodland rides, forest tracks and occasional pockets of heathland.
Park and Start: The Look Out Discovery Centre, Nine Mile Ride, Bracknell.
Start ref: SU 877662
Postcode: RG12 7QW
Public transport: First Beeline Buses operate 2 services (158 and 159) from Bracknell bus station to a Sainsbury store close to The Look Out (15 mins walk away).
Refreshments and facilities: The Look Out Discovery Centre.

It is also the UK Headquarters for BMW and the principal distribution centre for Waitrose.

1 From the Look Out car park, proceed towards The Discovery Centre, then bear half left through a children's play area.

The Look Out Discovery Centre has over 90 interactive science and nature exhibits, suitable for children of all ages. The exhibits are grouped into zones such as : Forces and Movement, Body and Perception, Sound and Communication.

2 At the Swinley Forest sign post, follow the Ramblers Route (half right), across an open area. The path swings to the left and then merges with the Heritage Trail (brown arrow).

Heritage trail near the Look Out

3 Continue to the next major fork, and then branch right along a wide sandy woodland ride. After a while, Gravel Hill will appear through the pine trees to your left.

The predominant tree species in the forest is conifer: Scots and Corsican pine. Various broadleaf species (birch, sweet chestnut and oak) can also be found on heathland and woodland edge habitats.

Gravel Hill cloaked in pine trees

4 At the next junction, go right (along the Heritage Trail) and pass Forest Pond on the left. Keep on this undulating track for 800 metres,

Caesar's Camp is the site of an Iron Age hillfort, built between 700 and 500 BC. Despite the name, this large defensive structure made up of ditches and banks in an 'oakleaf' outline, has no connection with the Roman Emperor.

Woodland ride leading to Caesar's Camp

until you reach Caesar's Camp (an Iron Age hillfort).

5 Go immediately left, to follow the power lines, in the direction of Star Posts. Cross a number of junctions, and pass a fenced-off reservoir, before reaching an eight-way junction – the Upper Star Post.

6 Keep ahead in the direction of the Lower Star Post, with power lines to your left.

7 When you reach the Lower Star Post – the trickiest junction of the walk, and the one with the most exits – keep following the power lines, along a wide flinty track, which rises and falls, before reaching a junction.

The Upper Star Post

8 Go right here, through a woodland glade, with an open area on the right. When you reach the 'MOD training area' sign, go left and then keep ahead at the next

The Lower Star Post

three-pronged fork, to follow the blue waymarked path.

9 The path ascends gradually with open area on left and then swings round to the right. Maintain direction as track merges from right, cross a junction, and keep ahead towards a large transmission mast.

10 Turn left at next junction along a broad track, and maintain direction, after 100 metres, to follow blue waymarked path, with a 'No motor vehicles' warning sign. The large transmission mast (a TV and radio relay station) now looms large, to the right.

11 Turn left when you reach a

Clearing near Bagshot Heath

concrete bunker, and go left again when the track splits, on a rising path. At the summit, there are fine views to the right through the Scots pines. Soon afterwards, the track plunges steeply downhill.

12 When you reach the bottom, go right through the fence at the earliest opportunity, to join a wider sandy track. Keep going, in a northerly direction, on a rising path, which swings to the right, before reaching Surrey Hills Reservoir.

13 Maintain direction along a track (as wide as a motorway), with spectacular views northwards. Descend steeply to another junction, and then keep ahead on a broad undulating track, which has been patched up, in places, with bright golden sand. Keep following signs for the Look Out. Eventually, you'll see cars passing ahead along the busy A322.

Large transmission mast near Bagshot

14 About 250 metres before a green barrier and the A322, go half left at a signpost in the direction of the Look Out. Keep ahead, past the 'Go Ape' assault course, until you reach the car park where the walk began.

Cycling in Swinley Forest along forest rides or in the mountain bike area is by permit only. These permits help pay for Public Liability insurance cover, and forest and trail upkeep.